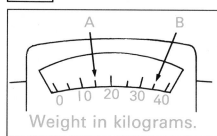

Each mark on the scale shows 5 kilograms.

A shows 15 kilograms.

B shows 35 kilograms.

Weight in kilograms.

1

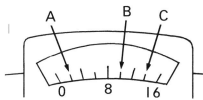

Weight in kilograms.

Each mark on the scale shows 2 kilograms.
What do these letters show?

(a) A   (b) B   (c) C

2

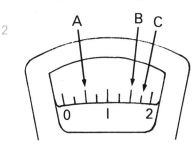

This is a parking meter.
There is a needle which shows the number
of hours left.
(Each small mark shows $\frac{1}{4}$ of an hour.)
How much time is left if the needle is

(a) at A   (b) at B   (c) at C?

3

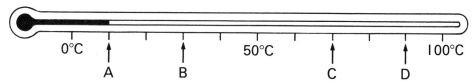

The thermometer shows the temperature in degrees Celsius.
(° means degrees, C stands for Celsius.)
Each mark shows 10°C.
What temperature is shown

(a) at A   (b) at B   (c) at C   (d) at D?

4

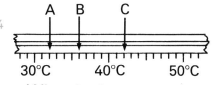

The picture shows part of a thermometer.

What is the temperature   (a) at A   (b) at B   (c) at C?

(d) How much does the temperature rise if it goes from A to B?

(e) How much does the temperature fall if it goes from C to A?

Hours and minutes.

There are 60 minutes in one hour.
The examples show different ways to tell the time.

2:30

We can say 'two thirty',
or 'thirty minutes past two',
or 'half past two'.

10:15

We can say 'ten fifteen',
or 'fifteen minutes past ten',
or 'quarter past ten'.

6:20

We can say 'six twenty',
or 'twenty minutes past six'.

9:28

We can say 'nine twenty-eight',
or 'twenty-eight minutes
past nine'.

Write each time in two ways.

(a) six _ten_

(b) ten minutes
   past six

1

(a) two _____

(b) twenty-five minutes
   _____

2

(a) eleven _____

(b) fifteen minutes
   _____

3

(a) nine _____

(b) five minutes
_____

4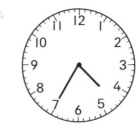

(a) four _____

(b) thirty-five minutes
_____

5

(a) seven _____

(b) forty-five minutes

6

(a) twelve _____

(b) _____ minutes past twelve

7

(a) one _____

(b) _____ minutes past one

Find the right answers.
For example the first answer is 8 (f) 4:12, twelve minutes past four.

8   4:12
9   4:50
10 3:45
11 3:48
12 5:10
13 4:08

(a) ten minutes past five
(b) forty-five minutes past three
(c) eight minutes past four
(d) four fifty
(e) three forty-eight
(f) twelve minutes past four

a.m. and p.m.

There are 60 seconds in one minute.

There are 60 minutes in one hour.

There are 24 hours in one day.

The second hand goes around once in one minute.

The minute hand goes around once in one hour.

The hour hand goes around twice in one day.

The letters a.m. are used for times after 12:00 midnight and before 12:00 noon.

The letters p.m. are used for times after 12:00 noon and before 12:00 midnight.

Daylight or dark?
Examples: 2:15 a.m. dark   3:25 p.m. daylight.

1 12:00 midnight	2 12:00 noon	3 3:00 a.m.	4 3:00 p.m.
5 11:45 p.m.	6 11:45 a.m.	7 2:36 a.m.	8 2:36 p.m.
9 10:30 a.m.	10 10:30 p.m.	11 1:10 a.m.	12 1:10 p.m.

How many:

13   hours in a day?

14   minutes in an hour?

15   seconds in a minute?

16   seconds in two minutes?

17   minutes in quarter of an hour?

18   minutes in a half hour?

Use a.m. or p.m. in your answers.
What time did you (or will you):

19   get up today?

20   eat breakfast?

21   leave for school?

22   arrive at school?

23   have morning break?

24   start afternoon school?

25   have afternoon break?

26   finish school?

27   get home?

28   go to bed?

1 45p +27p	2 62p +19p
3 38p +38p	4 46p +62p
5 74p +46p	6 76p +18p
7 64p −39p	8 80p −42p
9 80p −54p	10 86p −35p

More about time.

Maria woke up at She had to be in school at

How much time did she have?

Here are two ways to get the answer.

Wake-up time				School time
7:15	I hour ⟹	8:15	I5 minutes ⟹	8:30

I hour and I5 minutes

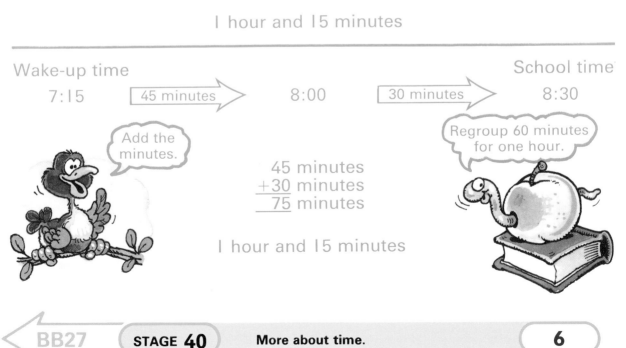

Wake-up time				School time
7:15	45 minutes ⟹	8:00	30 minutes ⟹	8:30

Add the minutes.

```
 45 minutes
+30 minutes
 75 minutes
```

I hour and I5 minutes

Regroup 60 minutes for one hour.

Give the time that is:

1. 25 minutes later than 3:00.
2. 40 minutes later than 10:05.
3. 20 minutes later than 3:10.
4. 10 minutes later than 8:45.
5. 5 minutes later than 2:35.
6. 15 minutes later than 2:20.
7. 23 minutes later than 11:15.
8. 16 minutes later than 4:28.
9. 10 minutes earlier than 8:25.
10. 15 minutes earlier than 6:47.
11. 10 minutes earlier than 9:40.
12. 20 minutes earlier than 11:30.
13. 30 minutes earlier than 3:48.
14. 8 minutes earlier than 6:15.

How many minutes from:

15. 8:10 to 8:40?
16. 1:17 to 1:50?
17. 10:38 to 10:55?
18. 7:50 to 7:59?
19. 2:25 to 2:50?
20. 9:15 to 9:37?
21. 4:15 to 5:15?
22. 1:05 to 2:00?
23. 6:20 to 7:00?
24. 1:30 to 2:50?
25. 4:20 to 5:50?
26. 7:10 to 8:20?
27. 7:45 to 8:30?
28. 10:30 to 11:10?
29. 1:50 to 2:35?

30. School begins at 8:20. Susan got to school at 8:05. How many minutes early was she?

31. The television programme started at 7:30. Mark turned it on at 7:45. How many minutes did he miss?

32. John left for the match at 7:45. He arrived at 8:10. How long did it take him to get there?

33. Julie started raking leaves at 4:15. She finished at 5:00. How long did she work?

Shopping, with change.

Beans
28p

Cake
19p

Meat paste
17p

Tomato sauce
64p

Debbie bought a cake.

She gave the shopkeeper 50p.

He gave her the cake and said '19p'.

He gave her and said '20p'.

He gave her and said '40p'.

He gave her and said '50p'.

Discuss the shopkeeper's method of giving change with your teacher, or explain it to a friend.

---

1 Rick bought a tin of beans.
He gave the shopkeeper

  .

(a) How much did he give the shopkeeper?

(b) How much change did he get?

2 Jessica bought the meat paste.
She gave the shopkeeper

  .

(a) How much did she give the shopkeeper?

(b) How much change did she get?

3 Terry bought the tomato sauce. How much change would he get from

(a)

(b)

(c)

There are several ways of finding the **change**.

A   The shopkeeper's method as on page 8.

B   By subtraction.

C   By using a calculator.

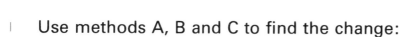

$$50p$$
$$-38p$$
$$\overline{12p}$$

I   Use methods A, B and C to find the change:

You have   (a) 50p and spend 38p.   (b) 90p and spend 76p.

(c) 40p and spend 19p.   (d) 80p and spend 71p.

(e) Which method did you find quickest?

(f) Which method gave the fewest mistakes?

2   Use any two of the methods A, B and C to find the change after buying these cakes.

Cost of cake	35p	20p	16p	48p	7p
Amount given to shop-keeper	50p	50p	20p	50p	20p
Change	15p				

3   Andrew bought a note book for 26p. He was given 14p change. How much did he give the shopkeeper?

4   Jessica bought a pen for 9p and a ruler for 26p. She gave the shopkeeper 50p.

(a) How much did Jessica spend?

(b) How much change did she get?

$+$, $-$, $\times$, or $\div$?

Sniff the hedgehog has put his muddy feet where the numbers should be.

Your answer to each question will be **add**, **subtract**, **multiply** or **divide**.

1 There are ⬛ boys and ⬛ girls.
How many children altogether?

2 ⬛ cows and ⬛ sheep.
How many more cows than sheep?

3 ⬛ chairs in each row.
⬛ rows.
How many chairs?

4 ⬛ children share ⬛ biscuits equally.
How many biscuits will each child get?

5 Ruth has ⬛ pence.
Rob has ⬛ pence.
How much less does Rob have than Ruth?

6 A grocer sells ⬛ apples.
He sells ⬛ apples to each customer.
How many customers does he have?

7 ⬛ bananas.
Each banana costs ⬛ pence.
What is the total cost?

8 ⬛ aliens.
Each alien has ⬛ arms.
How many arms altogether?

9 Carol is ⬛ centimetres tall.
Janet is ⬛ centimetres tall.
How much taller is Carol than Janet?

10 The distance from Town A to Town B is ⬛ kilometres.
Mr Fletcher started at A and drove ⬛ kilometres towards B, and stopped.
How far was he from B?

You need to use a calculator to answer some of these questions.

Your answers to the questions on page 10 will help you.

1 There are 14 boys and 29 girls.
How many children altogether?

2 88 cows and 69 sheep.
How many more cows than sheep?

3 17 chairs in each row.
5 rows.
How many chairs?

4 3 children share 24 biscuits equally.
How many biscuits will each child get?

5 Ruth has 90 pence.
Rob has 49 pence.
How much less does Rob have than Ruth?

6 A grocer sells 96 apples.
He sells 8 apples to each customer.
How many customers does he have?

7 25 bananas.
Each banana costs 9 pence.
What is the total cost?

8 13 aliens.
Each alien has 6 arms.
How many arms altogether?

9 Carol is 152 centimetres tall.
Jane is 149 centimetres tall.
How much taller is Carol than Jane?

10 The distance between Town A and Town B is 160 kilometres.
Mr Fletcher started at A and drove 96 kilometres towards B, and stopped.
How far was he from B?

Games and picnics.

1 Going to a picnic.
   4 children in a car.
   8 cars.
   How many children?

2 People at picnic.
   28 children.
   4 adults.
   How many people?

3 Tug-of-War.
   3 teams.
   9 in each team.
   How many altogether?

4 Sack race.
   2 races.
   8 children in each race.
   How many children?

5 Cricket and tennis.
   22 played cricket.
   19 played tennis.
   How many played?

6 Paper plates.
   5 plates per pack.
   6 packs.
   How many plates?

7 Biscuits.
   24 biscuits.
   3 children.
   How many biscuits each?

8 Drinking cups.
   9 packs of 5 cups each.
   40 people.
   How many cups left over?

9 Sandwiches.
10 sandwiches per box.
9 boxes.
How many sandwiches?

10 Races.
40 children run in races.
5 children in each race.
How many races?

11 Lemon squash.
Made 80 cups.
Drank 66 cups.
How many cups left?

12 Going home.
40 people.
4 in each car.
How many cars?

1 How many minutes from:

(a) 1:20 to 1:53?   (b) 3:17 to 3:50?   (c) 7:09 to 7:41?

(d) 10:20 to 11:00?   (e) 9:15 to 10:25?   (f) 5:30 to 7:00?

2 What is the time:

(a) 20 minutes after 4:10?   (b) 15 minutes after 1:50?

(c) 30 minutes before 8:42?   (d) 26 minutes before 12:30?

The music club.

1 Forming the band.
  19 brass players.
  23 woodwind players.
  6 drummers.
  How many children
  in the band?

2 Buying a trumpet.
  Cost £189.
  Have £115.
  How much more money
  is needed?

3 Giving out music sheets.
  8 players.
  10 sheets of music each.
  How many sheets of music?

4 Marching in a parade.
  36 children in the band.
  4 equal rows.
  How many in each row?

5 Hiring a flute.
  £3 per week.
  9 weeks.
  How much will this cost?

6 Setting up chairs.
  80 chairs.
  10 in each row.
  How many rows?

7 Selling programmes.
  5p for each programme.
  How much for:
  (a) 7 programmes?
  (b) 9 programmes?

8 Playing tunes.
  A tune takes 6 minutes.
  How many can be played
  in 1 hour?

Picture graph.

A class decided to raise money by collecting cans for 2 weeks.
They used a picture graph to show how many cans they collected.

Cans collected each day.			
First Week		**Second Week**	
Monday	🥫🥫🥫🥫	Monday	🥫🥫🥫🥫🥫🥫🥫
Tuesday	🥫🥫🥫🥫🥫🥫	Tuesday	🥫🥫🥫🥫🥫🥫🥫🥫
Wednesday	🥫🥫🥫	Wednesday	🥫🥫🥫🥫
Thursday	🥫🥫🥫🥫🥫🥫🥫	Thursday	🥫🥫🥫🥫🥫🥫🥫🥫🥫
Friday	🥫🥫🥫🥫🥫	Friday	🥫🥫🥫🥫🥫🥫

Each 🥫 stands for 8 cans.

1. On what day were the fewest cans collected?

2. On what day were the most cans collected?

3. How many cans were collected on the first day?

4. How many cans were collected on the last day?

5. How many were collected on the first two days?

6. Were more collected on the first Thursday or the second Thursday? How many more?

7. In the first week, how many cans were collected each day?

8. What was the total number of cans collected in the first week?

9. In the second week, how many cans were collected each day?

10. What was the total number of cans collected in the second week?

11. How many cans were collected during the two weeks?

12. How many more cans were collected in the second week than in the first week?

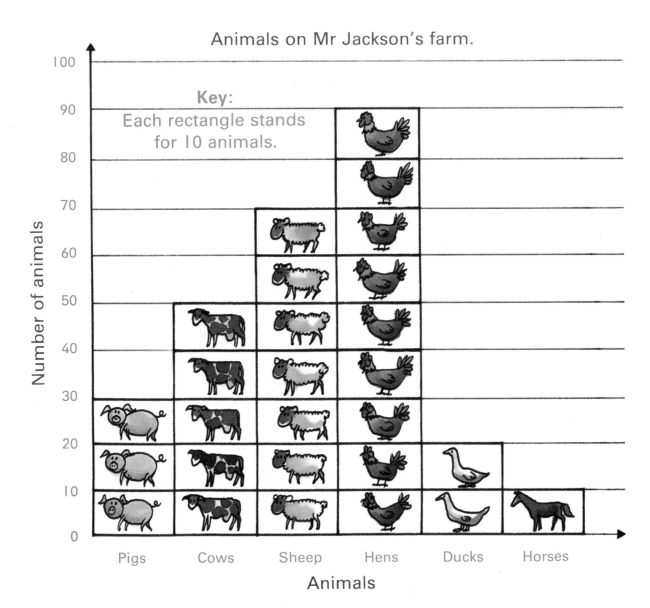

Animals on Mr Jackson's farm.

Key: Each rectangle stands for 10 animals.

1 How many:
   (a) pigs? (b) cows? (c) sheep?
   (d) hens? (e) ducks? (f) horses?

2 How many animals altogether?

3 How many more:
   (a) hens than sheep?
   (b) pigs than horses?

4 How many more cows must Mr Jackson buy so that he will have 100?

5 Mr Jackson sold 28 sheep. How many sheep were left?

6 He bought 19 more pigs. How many pigs altogether?

Eggs laid in one week.

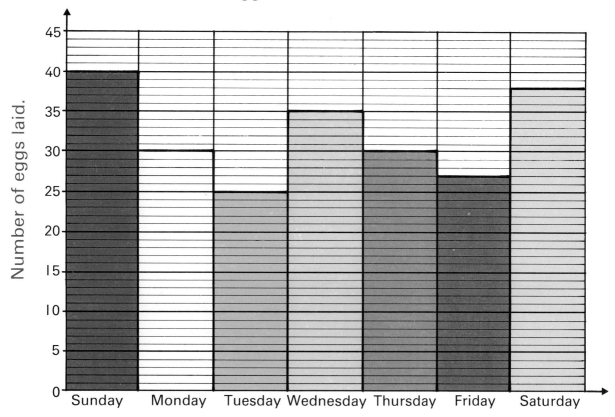

Number of eggs laid.

Days of the week.

1 How many eggs were laid on:
   (a) Sunday? (b) Monday? (c) Tuesday? (d) Wednesday?
   (e) Thursday? (f) Friday? (g) Saturday?

2 How many eggs were laid in the week?

3 On which day were most eggs laid?

4 On which day were the least number of eggs laid?

5 How many more eggs were laid on Sunday
   than on Saturday?

6 How many more eggs would have to be laid to
   make the number in the week 250?

7 What is the total number of eggs laid
   on Sunday, Monday and Tuesday?

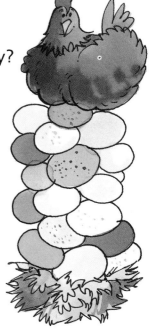

Fractions of shapes.

1 Which shapes show halves?

(a) 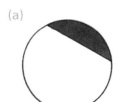   (b)    (c) 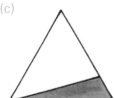   (d)

---

2 Which shapes show thirds?

(a)    (b) 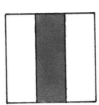   (c) 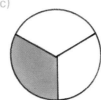   (d)

---

3 Which shapes show quarters?

(a) 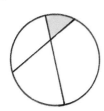   (b) 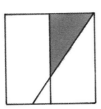   (c)    (d)

---

4 Draw a square.
   Colour $\frac{1}{2}$ red.

5 Draw a circle.
   Colour $\frac{1}{4}$ blue.

6 Draw a triangle.
   Colour $\frac{1}{2}$ green.

7 Draw a rectangle.
   Colour $\frac{1}{4}$ black.

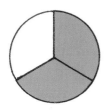 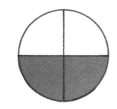 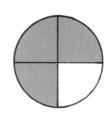

2 parts are blue   2 parts are red   3 parts are green
3 equal parts   4 equal parts   4 equal parts

Write the fraction that is coloured.

1

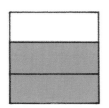

$\frac{1}{3}$ $\frac{1}{2}$ $\frac{2}{3}$

2

$\frac{1}{4}$ $\frac{2}{4}$ $\frac{3}{4}$

3

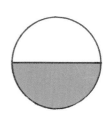

$\frac{1}{3}$ $\frac{1}{2}$ $\frac{1}{4}$

4

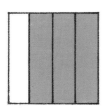

$\frac{1}{2}$ $\frac{2}{3}$ $\frac{3}{4}$

5

$\frac{1}{2}$ $\frac{1}{3}$ $\frac{3}{4}$

6

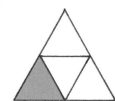

$\frac{1}{2}$ $\frac{1}{3}$ $\frac{1}{4}$

7

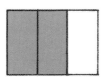

$\frac{1}{2}$ $\frac{2}{3}$ $\frac{3}{4}$

8

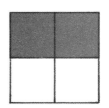

$\frac{1}{3}$ $\frac{2}{4}$ $\frac{2}{3}$

9

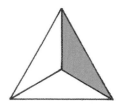

$\frac{1}{2}$ $\frac{1}{3}$ $\frac{1}{4}$

For each shape write (a) the fraction that is coloured,

and (b) the fraction that is **not** coloured.

(a) $\frac{3}{4}$　　(b) $\frac{1}{4}$

1 　　2 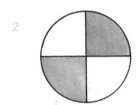　　3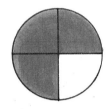

4 　　5 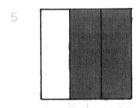　　6

7 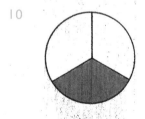　　8 　　9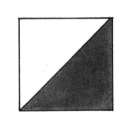

10 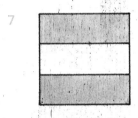　　11 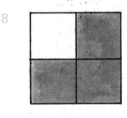　　12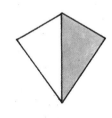

13 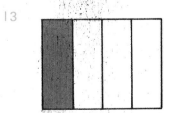　　14 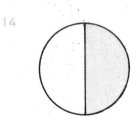　　15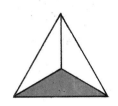

More fractions.

For each set write (a) the fraction in the loop,
and (b) the fraction **not** in the loop.

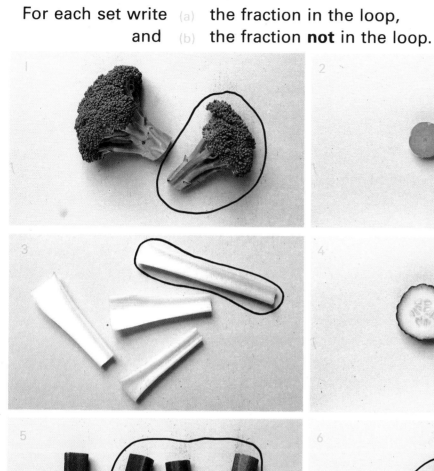

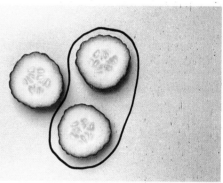

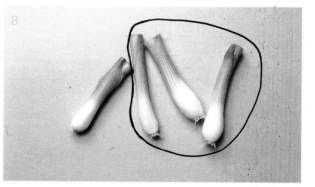

Write the fraction for each colour.

1

(a) red ____   (b) green ____

2

(a) red ____   (b) yellow ____

3

(a) yellow ____   (b) green ____

4

(a) orange ____   (b) green ____

5

(a) red ____   (b) green ____

6

(a) yellow ____   (b) red ____

7

(a) orange ____   (b) yellow ____

8

(a) red ____   (b) green ____

9

(a) red ____   (b) green ____   (c) yellow ____

Mental arithmetic.

```
   46        68        81        59        33        77
 +  9      +  9      +  9      +  9      +  9      +  9
   55        77        90        68        42        86
```

To add 9 you could add 10, then subtract 1.

That's right, because $9 = 10 - 1$

To add 29 you could add 30, then subtract 1. $29 = 30 - 1$

To add 48 you could add 50 and subtract 2. $48 = 50 - 2$

Use the methods above to do these in your head.

1 Add 9 to   (a) 14   (b) 27   (c) 39   (d) 45   (e) 52

2 Add 29 to   (a) 13   (b) 26   (c) 38   (d) 47   (e) 53

3 Add 8 to   (a) 18   (b) 25   (c) 63   (d) 74   (e) 87

4 Add 38 to   (a) 16   (b) 29   (c) 35   (d) 44   (e) 53

To subtract 9 you could subtract 10, then add 1.

Yes. Because when you subtract 10 you've subtracted 1 too many, so you must add 1.

5 Subtract 9 from   (a) 23   (b) 38   (c) 51   (d) 84   (e) 92

6 Subtract 19 from   (a) 28   (b) 40   (c) 55   (d) 64   (e) 76

7 Subtract 49 from   (a) 54   (b) 61   (c) 74   (d) 85   (e) 97

Input and output

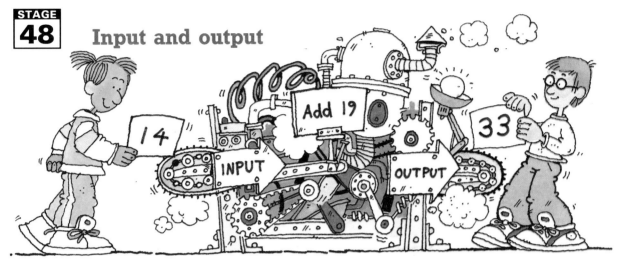

INPUT is what is put into the machine.
OUTPUT is what comes out of the machine.

The machine adds 19 to the INPUT.
If 28 was the INPUT the OUTPUT would be 47   (28 + 19 = 47).

1   Copy and complete.

(a)

Add 6	
INPUT	OUTPUT
23	
17	
19	
34	

(b)

Add 20	
INPUT	OUTPUT
18	
25	
30	
46	

(c)

Add 35	
INPUT	OUTPUT
21	
8	
47	
59	

2   Copy and complete.

(a)

Subtract 7	
INPUT	OUTPUT
15	
22	
48	
50	

(b)

Subtract 12	
INPUT	OUTPUT
19	
35	
61	
90	

(c)

Subtract 39	
INPUT	OUTPUT
56	
74	
82	
93	

 Add 5  OUTPUT 13

The machine is set to 'add 5'.
The **output** is 13. What is the **input**?

What number can we add 5 to and get 13?

8, because 8 + 5 = 13

Another way is to subtract 5 from 13. 13 − 5 = 8 so 8 + 5 = 13.

1 Copy and complete.

(a)

Add 4	
INPUT	OUTPUT
	7
	11
	20
	33

(b)

Add 10	
INPUT	OUTPUT
	50
	16
	31
	84

(c)

Add 14	
INPUT	OUTPUT
	24
	36
	41
	53

2 Copy and complete.

(a)

Subtract 3	
INPUT	OUTPUT
	8
	27
	54
	79

(b)

Subtract 20	
INPUT	OUTPUT
	40
	51
	66
	79

(c)

Subtract 17	
INPUT	OUTPUT
	13
	30
	45
	51

Symmetry.

Fold a sheet of paper in half.
Cut out a shape.
Start and finish on
the folded edge.
Open the shape you
have cut out.
The shape is symmetrical.

This line is called
the line of symmetry.

---

1. Is the dotted line a line of symmetry?

(a) 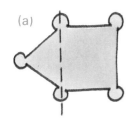 (b) (c) 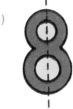 (d)

(e) 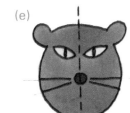 (f)  (g)  (h)

2. Trace these shapes.
Draw the missing part to make them symmetrical.

(a) (b) (c) (d)

(e) (f) (g) (h)

(i) (j) (k) (l)

1 The pattern is symmetrical
about the line of symmetry.
Copy it on to
centimetre-squared paper.
Add other coloured squares
to both sides so the pattern
is still symmetrical.

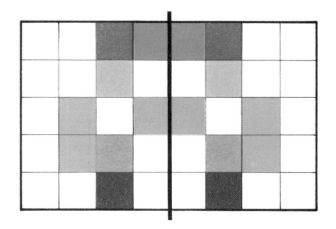

2 Copy and complete this pattern so that it is symmetrical.

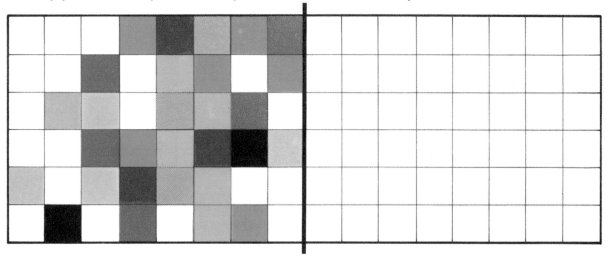

3 Copy and complete this pattern so that it is symmetrical.

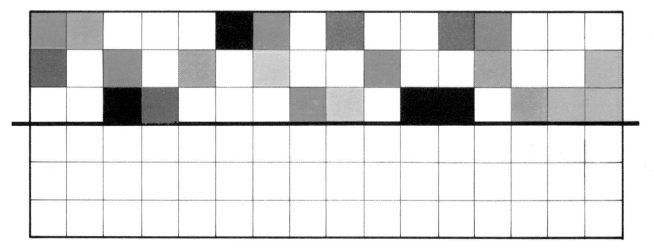

3D Symmetry.

A **plane** is a flat surface, such as this page or a blackboard.

The orange has been cut in half.
Both parts are exactly the same.
The red plane is called a **plane of symmetry**.

Answer **yes** if the plane is a plane of symmetry.
Answer **no** if it is not a plane of symmetry.

1

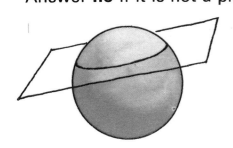

2

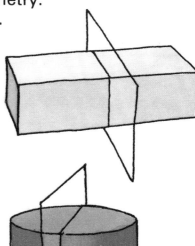

3

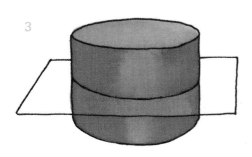

4

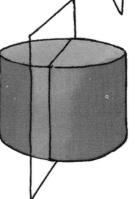

Which shapes have half shaded?

(a)   (b)   (c)   (d)

STAGE 51 — Division with remainders.

Some divisions do not come out evenly.

cakes on
each plate → 2)9 ← cakes
−8 ·○ (2 × 4)
1 ← cake left over

cakes on
2 ← each plate
plates → 4)9 ← cakes
−8 ·○ (4 × 2)
1 ← cake left over

The 1 that is left over is called the **remainder**. The remainder is always less than the number we are dividing by.

The remainder is 1.

2 R1
4)9
−8
1

Copy and complete.

Find the remainder.

2R 2
3)8
−6
2

3R
2)7
−6
—

3R
4)14
−12
—

9R
5)49
−45
—

6R
7)45
−42
—

4R
6)29
−24
—

5R
8)43
−40
—

5R
9)50
−45
—

7R
8)60
−56
—

5R
7)39
−35
—

1 Copy and complete.

(a) $5 \overline{) 29}$ (b) $3 \overline{) 20}$ (c) $2 \overline{) 17}$ (d) $5 \overline{) 27}$ (e) $4 \overline{) 30}$

(f) $5 \overline{) 50}$ (g) $10 \overline{) 43}$ (h) $4 \overline{) 37}$ (i) $3 \overline{) 25}$ (j) $4 \overline{) 35}$

(k) $10 \overline{) 46}$ (l) $5 \overline{) 35}$ (m) $10 \overline{) 45}$ (n) $4 \overline{) 20}$ (o) $10 \overline{) 67}$

2 Solve.

(a) 26 players.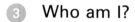
4 in a team.
How many teams?
How many players left over?

(b) 47 apples.
5 in a bag.
How many bags?
How many apples left over?

(c) 48 tyres.
5 for each lorry.
How many lorries?
How many tyres left over?

(d) 43 chairs.
5 in each row.
How many rows?
How many chairs left over?

(e) 35 flowers.
10 in each bunch.
How many bunches?
How many flowers left over?

(f) 52 school days.
5 in each school week.
How many school weeks?
How many days left over?

3 Who am I?

(a) If you divide me by 2, you get 5 and a remainder of 1.

(b) If you divide me by 10, you get 3 and a remainder of 7.

(c) I am less than 20. If you divide me by 5, you get a remainder of 2. If you divide me by 3, you get a remainder of 2.

Division discoveries

Ann, Brian and Carol used their calculators to divide numbers.
This is what they discovered.

> If a number divides exactly by 2 the units digit is always 0, 2, 4, 6 or 8.

> So if the units digit is *not* 0, 2, 4, 6 or 8 there is a remainder when you divide by 2.

> If a number divides exactly by 5 the units digit is always 0 or 5.

> So if the units digit is *not* 5 or 0 there is a remainder when you divide by 5.

> If a number divides exactly by 10 the units digit is always 0.

> So if the units digit is *not* 0 there is a remainder when you divide by 10.

---

1 Use the rules above to decide which of these numbers do *not* have a remainder when divided by 2.

   (a) 14   (b) 20   (c) 17   (d) 34   (e) 48   (f) 53   (g) 76

   Check your answers by using a calculator.

2 Which of these *do* have a remainder when divided by 5?

   (a) 15   (b) 19   (c) 24   (d) 30   (e) 36   (f) 40   (g) 63

   Check your answers by using a calculator.

3 Answer **'remainder'** or **'no remainder'** for when the numbers are divided by 10.

   (a) 10   (b) 25   (c) 40   (d) 72   (e) 95   (f) 100   (g) 160

   Check your answers by using a calculator.

14 sweets can be put in sets of 2 with nothing left over.
That means 14 ÷ 2 does not have a remainder.

We say that 14 can be divided exactly by 2.

'Divide exactly' means there is no remainder.

That means that 14 is an **even** number.

If a number divides exactly by 2 it is **even**. If it does not divide exactly by 2 it is **odd**.

1   Use the rule from page 31 to find if these numbers are **even** or **odd**.

(a) 7   (b) 18   (c) 23   (d) 47   (e) 68   (f) 74

(g) 96   (h) 109   (i) 134   (j) 216   (k) 943   (l) 1082

2   Use a calculator to find if these numbers are **even** or **odd**.

(a) 9   (b) 17   (c) 22   (d) 39   (e) 54   (f) 67

(g) 88   (h) 106   (i) 132   (j) 261   (k) 700   (l) 1383

3   Play this car number game with a friend:

Write down the car numbers as cars pass you.
You score 1 for each odd number.

Your friend scores 1 for each even number.
521 is odd so you score 1.

The first to score 20 wins.

Sharing.

Mark and Carol share 5 cakes equally.

Mark has 2 cakes. Carol has 2 cakes.

I cake is left.
They cut that cake in half.
They have one half each.

They each have $2\frac{1}{2}$ cakes.

$$5 \div 2 = 2\frac{1}{2}$$

1 Divide by 2. How many each?

(a)   (b)

(c)

2 Divide these numbers by 2. Draw pictures to help, if you want to.

(a) 13   (b) 11   (c) 19   (d) 21   (e) 18

3 Think: how is the work on this page connected to odd and
even numbers? See if you can explain to a friend.

STAGE
54 **More problems.**

These steps can help you solve problems.

A Read the problem and find the question.

Matthew had 40 strawberry plants. He planted 10 in each row. How many rows did he plant?

B What are the facts?

40 strawberry plants, 10 in each row.

C Decide what to do.

Add, subtract, multiply, or divide?

D Answer the question.

$$10 \overline{)\, 40}^{\,4}$$

He planted 4 rows.

E Does your answer seem right?

There are 4 rows of 10. That makes 40 plants.

The answer seems right.

Use the steps to help you work out these problems:

2 Julie spent 65p on carrot seeds, 48p on radish seeds, and 85p on tomato plants. How much did she spend?

4 Mr Johnson had 42 bulbs. He bought two more bags. There were 30 bulbs in a bag. How many bulbs did he have altogether?

1 Mrs Johnson bought a hose for £9.45. She gave the shop assistant £10. How much change did she get?

3 Matthew had £4. He bought some bean plants for 65p and some tomato plants for 35p. How much money did he have left?

5 The shop had 4 cabbage plants in each tray. The Johnsons decided to buy 24 plants. How many trays did they buy?

6   Julie and Matthew planted
    3 rows of tomato plants with
    9 plants in each row.
    How many did they plant?

7   Julie planted 10 rows of cucumber.
    She put 7 seeds in each row.
    How many cucumber seeds
    did she plant?

8   Matthew planted 45 onions.
    He planted 5 rows with the
    same number of onions
    in each row. How many did
    he plant in each row?

9   Julie has 20 lettuce plants.
    She wants to plant them in
    rows of 3.

    (a)   How many rows will she
          have?

    (b)   How many plants are left
          over?

10 Julie bought 24 plants. $\frac{1}{4}$ of
    them were flower plants, the
    rest were vegetable plants.

    (a)   What fraction were
          vegetables?

    (b)   How many flower plants
          did she buy?

    (c)   How many vegetable
          plants did she buy?

11 Matthew had 50p. He bought
    3 packets of seeds. Each packet
    cost 8p.

    (a)   How much did the seeds
          cost altogether?

    (b)   How much money did he
          have left?

12 A tray of 10 pansies costs
    £0.70. What is the cost of:

    (a)   1 pansy?

    (b)   6 pansies?

    (c)   9 pansies?

13 Mrs Jones spent $\frac{1}{3}$ of her
    money on a bird table.
    The table cost £9.

    (a)   How much money did she
          have before she bought
          the table?

    (b)   How much money did she
          have left after buying the
          table?

Negative numbers.

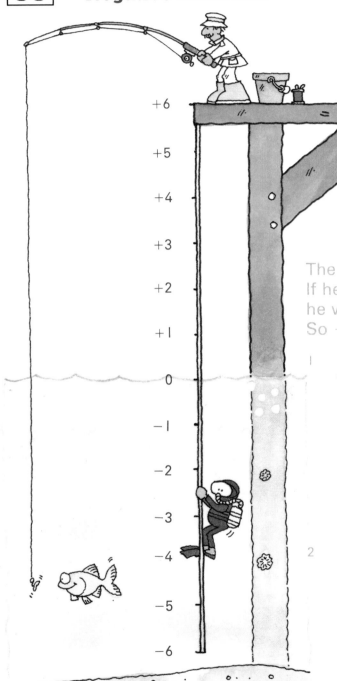

up (add)

down (subtract)

+6
+5
+4
+3
+2
+1
0
−1
−2
−3
−4
−5
−6

The frogman's feet are on −4.
If he goes up 2 (+2) rungs
he will be on −2.
So −4 + 2 = −2.

1 Give the number the frogman
finishes on.
He starts at −4 each time.
He goes:

(a) up 5   (b) up 7

(c) up 4   (d) up 8

(e) down 1   (f) down 2

2 Start on +3, finish on +5.
How far have you moved up or
down?   Up 2.

(a) Start on +1 finish on −3

(b) Start on −5 finish on 0

(c) Start on 0 finish on +6

3 Use the ladder to answer these questions.

−1 + 2 = +1   (a) +3 +2 = ___   (b) −6 +4 = ___   (c) 0 + 5 = ___

(d) +2 −2 = ___   (e) +4 −5 = ___   (f) −1 −3 = ___   (g) −2 −1 = ___

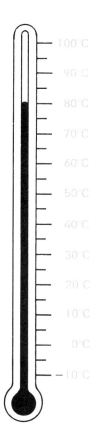

Temperature is measured in degrees Celsius.
This thermometer shows 80°C.
We say 'eighty degrees Celsius'.

Water boils at 100°C
Water freezes at 0°C

1 The temperature of some water is 80°C.
What will it be if it

(a) goes up 17°?   (b) goes up 20°?

(c) goes down 10°?   (d) goes down 50°?

(e) goes down 80°?   (f) goes down 90°?

Temperatures can go above 100°C and
below the −10°C shown on the thermometer.

Here is a thermometer for temperatures between 30°C and −35°C.

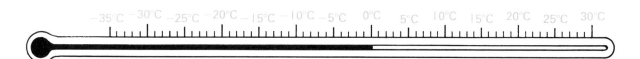

2 What is the temperature if it

(a) starts at −20°C and goes down 5°C?

(b) starts at 5°C and goes down 10°C?

(c) starts at −35°C and goes up 15°C?

(d) starts at −20°C and goes up 20°C?

3 Write how many degrees up or down the temperature goes from:

(a) −15°C to +5°C   (b) 13°C to 20°C   (c) 0°C to −8°C

(d) −2°C to −9°C   (e) 10°C to −1°C   (f) −18°C to −31°C

(g) −19°C to 0°C

Centimetres.

The **centimetre (cm)** is a unit for measuring length in the metric system.

The length of the nail is between 5 and 6 centimetres. It is nearer to 6 centimetres. The length of the nail (measured to the nearest centimetre) is 6 centimetres.

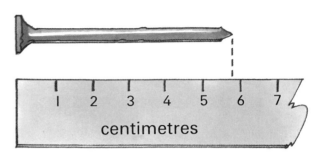

centimetres

I   Measure to the nearest centimetre.

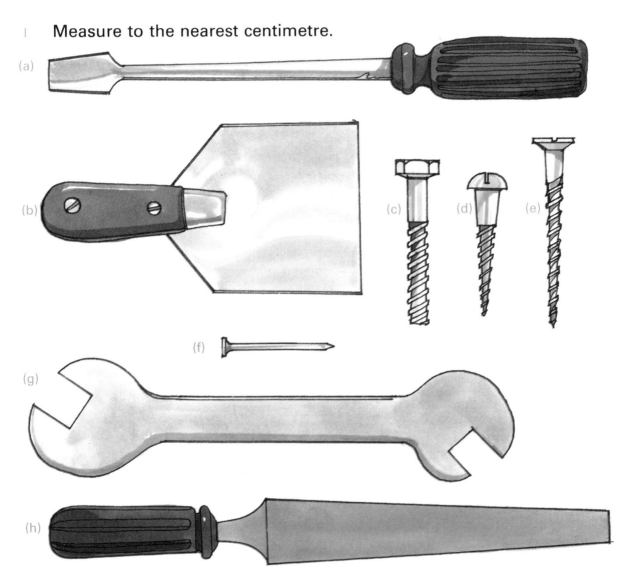

(a)

(b)

(c)

(d)

(e)

(f)

(g)

(h)

2   Draw lines these lengths:

(a) 9 cm   (b) 14 cm   (c) 18 cm   (d) 11 cm

---

3   Draw a line that has a length between:

(a) 8 cm and 9 cm, but nearer 8 cm.

(b) 6 cm and 7 cm, but nearer 7 cm.

---

4   Measure to the nearest centimetre:

(a) the length of your little finger,

(b) the breadth of your hand,

(c) the length of your foot,

(d) around your wrist,
     (if you don't have a
     centimetre tape measure,
     use string and a ruler.)

(e) around your waist,

(f) your height,

(g) the sides of this book,

(h) the length of your table,

(i) the breadth of your table,

(j) the length of your pencil,

(k) the height of your chair.

Metres and kilometres.

The **metre (m)** is used to
measure longer lengths
in the metric system.
If you took a 'giant step',
it would be close to
1 metre long.

1 metre (m) = 100 cm

1   Measure to the nearest metre:

(a)   the length of your classroom,

(b)   the breadth of your classroom,

(c)   the height of a table,

(d)   the breadth of the door,

(e)   the width of a window,

(f)   the longest side of the blackboard,

(g)   the length of the hall,

(h)   the breadth of the hall.

2   Copy and complete:

(a)   1 m = ____ cm

(b)   3 m = ____ cm

(c)   5 m = ____ cm

(d)   8 m = ____ cm

(e)   10 m = ____ cm

(f)   200 cm = ____ m

(g)   400 cm = ____ m

(h)   700 cm = ____ m

(i)   1000 cm = ____ m

(j)   1 m 30 cm = ____ cm

(k)   1 m 60 cm = ____ cm

(l)   2 m 20 cm = ____ cm

(m)   150 cm = 1 m ____ cm

(n)   180 cm = 1 m ____ cm

(o)   210 cm = 2 m ____ cm

(p)   135 cm = ____ m ____ cm

(q)   215 cm = ____ m ____ cm

(r)   300 cm = ____ m ____ cm

The **kilometre (km)** is used to measure long distances in the metric system. If you took 1000 giant steps, you would have walked about 1 kilometre.

1 kilometre (km) = 1000 m

3 How many kilometres from:

(a) **Birmingham to Manchester?**

(b) **London to Exeter?**

(c) **Plymouth to Lincoln?**

(d) **Edinburgh to Newcastle?**

(e) **Leeds to Southampton?**

(f) **Liverpool to Bristol?**

4 Use your calculator to help you find the total distance in kilometres for these journeys:

(a) **Exeter → Bristol → Birmingham,**

(b) **Aberdeen → Glasgow → Edinburgh,**

(c) **Cardiff → Birmingham → Lincoln,**

(d) **Southampton → Lincoln → Manchester.**

5 (a) **1 km = _____ m**   (b) **4000 m = _____ km**

   (c) **2 km = _____ m**   (d) **3800 m = _____ km _____ m**

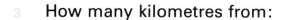

Project Lay out a 50 metre course on the school grounds or in the gym. Find out how long it takes you to walk 1 kilometre.

Perimeter.

The distance around a shape is called the **perimeter** of the shape.

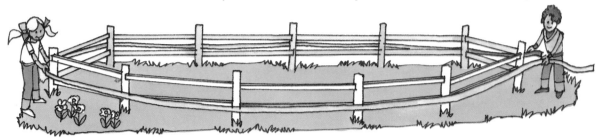

You can find the perimeter of a shape by adding the length of its sides.

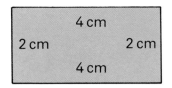

Perimeter = 4 cm + 2 cm + 4 cm + 2 cm = 12 cm

Give the perimeter of each figure.

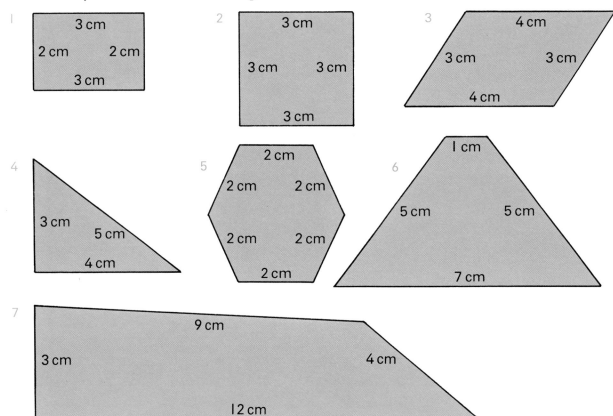

1
3 cm
2 cm   2 cm
3 cm

2
3 cm
3 cm   3 cm
3 cm

3
4 cm
3 cm   3 cm
4 cm

4
3 cm
5 cm
4 cm

5
2 cm
2 cm   2 cm
2 cm   2 cm
2 cm

6
I cm
5 cm   5 cm
7 cm

7
9 cm
3 cm   4 cm
12 cm

8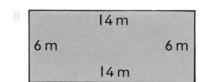

9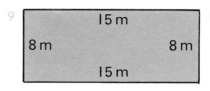

10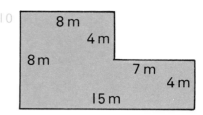

11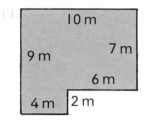

12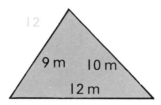

13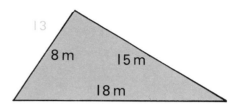

14 Measure the edges of a table top to the nearest centimetre. Find its perimeter.

15 Find the perimeter of a notice board in centimetres.

16 A garden is shaped like a rectangle. It is 42 m long and 26 m wide. How much fencing will be needed to go round it?

17 Complete this table for squares.

Length of each side in cm	1	2	3	4	5	6	7	8	9
Perimeter in cm									

keeping skills sharp

1 What fraction is: (a) red? (b) not red?

2 What fraction is:

(a) circles?
(b) triangles?

3 Find $\frac{1}{2}$ of 8.

4 Find $\frac{1}{3}$ of 12.

5 $\frac{1}{4}$ of 20 = _____

6 $\frac{1}{2}$ of 16 = _____

Find the perimeter of these shapes.

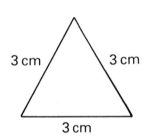

Perimeter = 3 cm × 3 = ___ cm

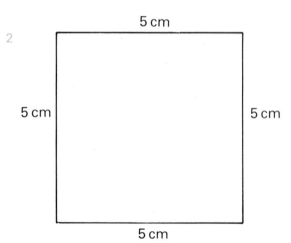

Perimeter = 5 cm × 4 = ___ cm

Perimeter = 4 cm × 5 = ___ cm

4   What is the perimeter of a six-sided shape if each side is 7 cm?

Measure the perimeter of these shapes.

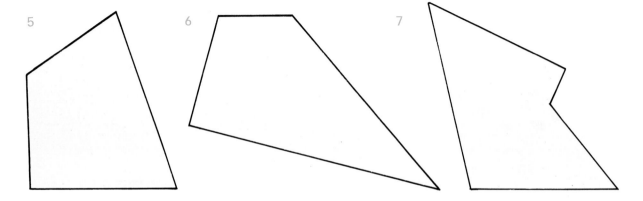

Measurement.

1 Measure your arm span and your height to the nearest centimetre.

2 Compare your measurements:

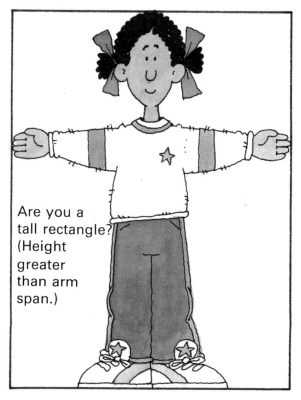

Are you a tall rectangle? (Height greater than arm span.)

Are you a square? (Height equals arm span.)

3 Find the number of children in your class who are squares, tall rectangles, and short rectangles.

4 Make a bar graph of what you found. For example:

Are you a short rectangle? (Height less than arm span.)

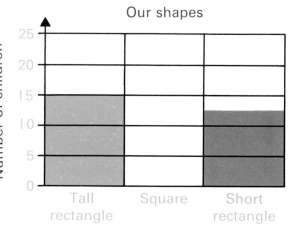

5 Write down some things that your graph shows.

1   Copy and complete this list of your measurements.

Name _____   Age _____

Weight in pounds _____ in kilograms_____

Height: in feet and inches _____

          in centimetres   _____   (see page 45)

Armspan: in feet and inches _____

          in centimetres   _____   (see page 45)

2   **a**   Estimate first then measure in centimetres:

     (a)   Distance round forehead _____

     (b)   Distance round neck   _____

     (c)   Distance round chest   _____

     (d)   Arm length   _____

     (e)   Handspan   _____

     (f)   Waist   _____

     (g)   Hips   _____

     (h)   Foot   _____

     (i)   Pace   _____

3   Which of **your** measurements would you use to get an approximate measurement of

     (a)   perimeter of the school

     (b)   height of a door   (c)   length of a room

     (d)   height of a room   (e)   distance round a table?

This small box has a volume of
I cubic centimetre.

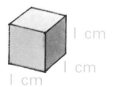

I cm
I cm
I cm

It will hold I **millilitre (ml)** of
water. The millilitre is used to
measure small amounts of liquid.

For measuring greater amounts,
the **litre (l)** is used.

I litre = I000 millilitres
            or
    I l = I000 ml

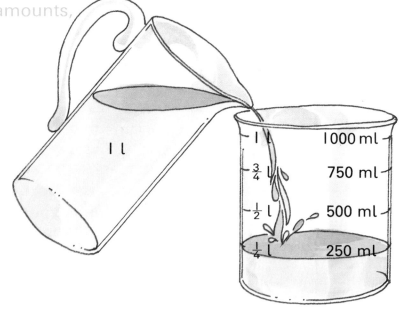

I l

I l   1000 ml

¾ l   750 ml

½ l   500 ml

¼ l   250 ml

Millilitre or litre?
Which unit would be used to measure:

1 the amount of medicine in
   a bottle?

2 the amount of petrol
   a car's tank holds?

3 the amount of water in
   a fish tank?

4 the juice of an orange?

Project 1   Make a list of things that are measured in litres.

Project 2   (a) Collect some containers and estimate how many
                      litres they will hold.

                 (b) Check your estimates by filling each container,
                      using a one litre jug.

Weight.

A **gram (g)** is used for weighing light things.
For weighing heavier things the **kilogram (kg)** is used.

  I kilogram (kg) = 1000 grams (g)

Would you use grams or kilograms to weigh:

1 yourself?	2 a pencil?	3 a crisp?	4 a car?
5 a sweet?	6 a bag of potatoes?	7 a ball of wool?	8 a pig?

Project 1 Collect at least five things you think weigh
about I kilogram. Weigh them. Record the weights
and see how good your guesses were.

Project 2 Weigh yourself in kilograms.

Project 3 Work with a group of friends. Find their weights.
Draw a bar graph to show their weights.
Make up some questions about your graph.
Give them to your friends to answer.

keeping skills sharp

You need a ruler and some string.
Measure to the nearest centimetre:

1    2    3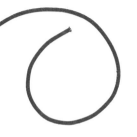

Graphs.

The picture graph shows how a class travelled to school.

How we came to school today.

Each ☺ stands for 2 children.

1 How many children walk?

2 How many children cycle?

3 How many children travel by car?

4 How many children travel by bus?

5 How many more walk than ride a bicycle?

6 How many children are there in the class?

7 How many do *not* walk to school?

8 How many children do these 'pin men' show? ☺☺☺

9 How many 'pin men' would be needed to show 20 children?

10 Draw a picture graph to show how your class travel to school.
Use ☺ to show one child.

Thirty children each named their two favourite books out of the five that the class liked best. They showed the results on a tally chart.

Book	Total
Charlie and the Chocolate Factory	‖‖‖‖‖‖‖‖
Stig of the Dump	‖‖‖‖‖‖‖
The Borrowers	‖‖‖‖‖‖
The Lion, the Witch and the Wardrobe	‖‖‖‖‖
Little Old Mrs Pepperpot	‖‖‖‖‖‖‖

1 Draw 🧍 to stand for 2 children. 8 pin men will be needed for *Charlie and the Chocolate Factory*.
How many pin men will you draw for:

(a) *Stig of the Dump*?   (b) *The Lion, the Witch and the Wardrobe*?

(c) *The Borrowers*?   (d) *Little Old Mrs Pepperpot*?

2 Draw a picture graph, like the one on page 49, to show the favourite books in question 1.

3 How many more votes did *Charlie and the Chocolate Factory* get than *Stig of the Dump*?

4 What was the total number of votes for *The Borrowers* and *Little Old Mrs Pepperpot*?

5 What is the difference in the number of votes for the most popular book and the least popular book?

6 What are the five most popular books for your class?

7 Make a tally chart as in question 1. Give each person in your class two votes. Don't forget to vote yourself.

8 Draw a picture graph, using pin men, to show the favourite books of your class. Use 🧍 to show one vote. Make up questions like questions 3, 4 and 5 then answer them.

Tables.

Egg production

	Sunday	Monday	Tuesday	Wednesday	Thursday	Friday	Saturday
Week 1	28	36	22	40	35	32	47
Week 2	50	55	49	63	47	62	54
Week 3	43	47	52	34	47	65	53
Week 4	72	81	69	80	75	67	84

The farmer wrote ☐ for every 20 eggs laid.
He wrote ⌈ for fewer than 20 eggs.
28 was written as ☐⌈ . 49 was written as ☐☐⌈ .

1   Draw ☐s and ⌈s to show the eggs laid:

   (a)   on each day in Week 4,   (b)   on each Monday,

   (c)   on Friday in Week 3.

2   On which day were   (a)   most eggs laid?

                        (b)   fewest eggs laid?

3   Use your calculator to find the total number of eggs laid in

   (a)   Week 1,   (b)   Week 2,   (c)   Week 3,   (d)   Week 4.

4   Use your calculator to find the total number of eggs laid on
   each day of the week.

Toss a coin. Does it show 'Heads' or 'Tails'?

 We will write H for 'head'. and T for 'tail'.

1 (a) Use one coin. Toss it twice.

The result could be H, T   or T, H   or H, H   or T, T.

Make a tally chart like the one below.
Record the results of your tosses on it.

First toss	Second toss	Tallies (put ✓ by *one* of these pairs of letters after every 2 throws)	Frequency (add up the ✓s)
H	T		
T	H		
H	H		
T	T		
		Total:	50

Keep tossing your coin two times, until you have made 100 tosses altogether (that is, 50 'goes').

(b) Do you think your coin is 'fair' or 'unfair'?
(Are there **about** 25 ticks for each pair of letters?)

(b) Stick some plasticine on one side of your coin.
Do another 100 tosses and make another chart.
Discuss the results with your teacher, or with another friend.

2   If a coin is tossed **three** times there are eight possible results.
They are:

HHH, HHT, HTT, TTT, TTH, THH, THT, HTH.

Make a 'tally' chart. Toss your coin until you have 40 'goes'
(that is 120 tosses altogether). Is your coin fair or unfair?
Discuss your results again with your teacher, or another friend.

You need a dice marked 1, 2, 3, 4, 5, 6.

1   If a 'fair' dice was rolled 60 times do you think it would show each number exactly 10 times?

2   (a)   Copy the tally chart below.

Roll your dice 60 times and record the results on your chart.

Number on dice	Tallies (Put a ✓ by one of these numbers after each throw)	Frequency (add up the ✓s)
1		
2		
3		
4		
5		
6		
	Total:	60

(b)   **Compare your answers in questions 1 and 2(a).
Do you think your dice is 'fair'?**

2   If two dice are thrown the smallest possible total of the numbers they show is 2.
The greatest possible number is 12.
Which of the possible totals 2, 3, 4, 5, 6, 7, 8, 9, 10, 11 or 12 do you think will appear most often in a large number of throws?
Work with some friends. Design a tally chart, and investigate the totals when two dice are thrown.

The months of the year.

1 January	2 February	3 March	4 April
5 May	6 June	7 July	8 August
9 September	10 October	11 November	12 December

1   Which is the first month?

2   What month is it now?

3   What is the next month?

4   What is the month before April?

5   Which is the eleventh month?

6   Which is the eighth month?

7   Which month comes after December?

8   Which month is your birthday in?

1 Copy and complete.

Monday		Wednesday		Friday		
1st	2nd	3rd	4th	5th	6th	7th

2 How many days are there (a) in one week

(b) in two weeks

(c) in one week, 4 days?

3 Which day is (a) three days after Monday

(b) two days after Saturday

(c) one day before Friday

(d) four days before Tuesday?

February, 1991

Mon	Tues	Wed	Thurs	Fri	Sat	Sun
				1	2	3
4	5	6	7	8	9	10
11	12	13	14	15	16	17
18	19	20	21	22	23	24
25	26	27	28			

4 (a) What is the date 5 days after February 16th?

(b) What day of the week is it?

5 (a) What is the date 4 days before February 10th?

(b) What day of the week is it?

6 It is February 5th. William's birthday is on February 21st. How many more days before his birthday?

Month	Number of days
1 January	31
2 February	28 or 29
3 March	31
4 April	30
5 May	31
6 June	30
7 July	31
8 August	31
9 September	30
10 October	31
11 November	30
12 December	31

Learn this rhyme:

30 days has September,
April, June and November.
All the rest have 31,
except for February alone.
Leap year coming once in four
gives to February one day more.

For years from 1901 to 1999 you can easily find which are leap years.
Divide the year by 4.
If there is no remainder it is a leap year.
$1984 \div 4 = 496$ so 1984 is a leap year
$1927 \div 4 = 481$ remainder 3 so 1927 is *not* a leap year.

1 **List the months** (a) **that have 30 days**

  (b) **that have 31 days**

2 **Use your calculator to find which of these are leap years.**

(a) 1924 (b) 1936 (c) 1942 (d) 1957 (e) 1988

(f) 1990 (g) 1906 (h) 1963 (i) 1970 (j) 1992

3 (a) **Is the present year a leap year?**

  (b) **When is the next leap year?**

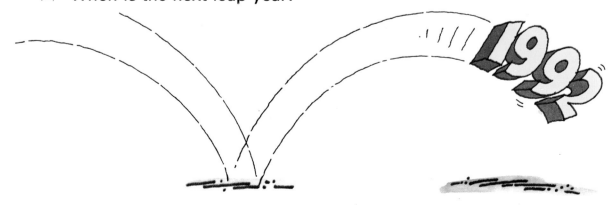

Points of the compass.

1 Draw a large circle. Cut it out.

Fold it in half.

Fold it in half again.

Fold it in half again.

Open it out and it will look like this:

Draw it on a piece of card and write the eight main points of the compass on it.

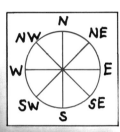

2

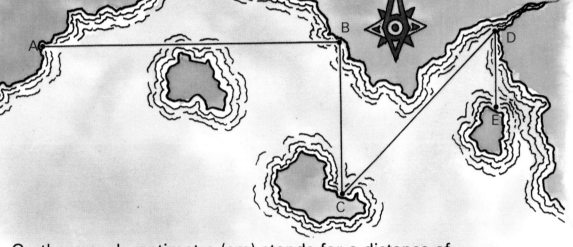

On the map I centimetre (cm) stands for a distance of I kilometre (km). What is the distance in kilometres from

(a) A to B,   (b) B to C,   (c) C to D,   (d) D to E?

What is the direction a ship travels in when it sails from

(e) A to B,   (f) B to C,   (g) C to D,   (h) D to E?

3   Use the map in question 2. A ship sails from E to A. What direction does it travel in when it sails from

(a) E to D,   (b) D to C,   (c) C to B,   (d) B to A?

Clockwise

The hands of a clock turn in this direction.
The direction is called **clockwise**.

Anti-clockwise

The opposite direction to clockwise
is called **anti-clockwise**.

Wind direction is named after the
direction the wind comes from.

This shows an east wind.

There are eight equal parts on this compass.
Each one is one eighth ($\frac{1}{8}$) of a
full turn.

Example
A wind from the east moves three eighths ($\frac{3}{8}$)
of a full turn in a clockwise direction.
What direction is it blowing from now? **Answer** SW.

1   Find the directions after these turns.

   (a)   from N clockwise through $\frac{3}{8}$ of a turn.

   (b)   from W anti-clockwise through $\frac{1}{8}$ of a turn.

   (c)   from NE clockwise through $\frac{1}{2}$ of a turn. ($\frac{1}{2}$ is the same as $\frac{4}{8}$).

   (d)   from NW anti-clockwise through $\frac{1}{4}$ of a turn. ($\frac{1}{4}$ is the same as $\frac{2}{8}$.)

2   How many eighths do you need to turn **clockwise** to move from SW to

   (a) NW,   (b) N,   (c) E,   (d) SE,   (e) S?

Some more problems.

1 Annie made 27 biscuits.
   She gave 3 biscuits to each friend.
   How many friends did she give biscuits to?

2 Sam had 78 stamps.
   Chandra had 59 stamps.

   (a) How many stamps did
        they have altogether?

   (b) How many more stamps
        did Sam have than Chandra?

3 Maggie bought 9 lollies.
   Each lolly cost 5p.
   How much did Maggie spend?

4 Liz had 82p.
   She bought a ribbon for 39p.
   How much did she have left?

5 **Half a litre of pop costs 46p.
   What is the cost of I litre?**

6 William has 40p.

   (a) How many chews can he buy?

   (b) How many bars of chocolate
        can he buy?

7 Peter bought six pencils costing 10p each
   and two rubbers costing 9p each.

   How much did he spend

   (a) on the pencils?

   (b) on the rubbers?

   (c) altogether?

These problems are like the ones on page 59, but the numbers are bigger.
You can use a calculator.

1　Annie made 176 biscuits. She gave 8 biscuits to each friend.
How many friends did she give biscuits to?

2　Sam had 305 stamps. Chandra had 187 stamps.

(a) How many stamps did they have altogether?

(b) How many more stamps did Sam have than Chandra?

3　Maggie bought 28 lollies. Each lolly cost 12p.
How much did Maggie spend?

4　Liz had £731. She bought some furniture for £567.
How much did she have left?

5　Half a kilogram of valuable metal costs £296.
What is the cost of a kilogram?

keeping skills sharp

1　What is the (a) seventh month of the year?

(b) eleventh month of the year?

2　How many days are there in February

(a) if it is not a leap year?　(b) if it is a leap year?

3　Which months have 30 days?

Check-up pages.

1   How many?

2   Write 879 in words.

3   How many?

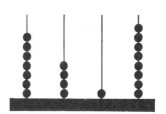

4   Write 3609 in words.

5   Write the number shown on the abacus

   (a)   in figures   (b)   in words.

6   Copy and complete by writing < or > instead of the ◯.

   (a)   99 ◯ 312   (b)   1234 ◯ 999

7   What number is   (a)   100   more than 6999   8   (a)   (2 + 8) + 9 =

                      (b)   1000 more than 6999   (b)   2 + (8 + 9) =

9   (a)   Add 3, 7, 6 and 4   (b)   Add 1, 8, 2, 9 and 5.

10 (a)   46   (b)   80   11   **65, 19**   Find   (a)   the sum
          + 39   − 27
                                                           (b)   the difference.

12 Copy and complete   (a)   11 + ___ = 26   (b)   ___ + 19 = 30.

13 Ben has 61p. Jessica has 49p.

    Find   (a)   the total amount they have.

           (b)   the difference in the amounts they have.

14 Copy and complete   156p = 100p + ___ p = £ ___ .

15 (a)   5 × 4   (b)   3 × 8   (c)   4 × 7   (d)   7 × 5

16 (a)   5 × 10   (b)   9 × 1   (c)   0 × 4   (d)   10 × 10

17 Pat has saved £65 towards buying a bicycle.
    The bicycle costs £93. How much more money does Pat need?

18 Jill had 9 apples. She used 6 of them, then picked 8 more.
    How many apples did she then have?

19 Each car carries 4 people. There are 20 people.
    How many cars are needed?

20 (a) 12 ÷ 2   (b) 18 ÷ 3   (c) 12 ÷ 4   (d) 20 ÷ 5

21 (a) (8 − 2) ÷ 3   (b) 4 + (4 × 4)   (c) (4 + 4) × 4

22 There are 10 potatoes in each bag.

    (a) How many potatoes in 6 bags?   (b) in 9 bags?

    (c) How many bags are needed for 70 potatoes?

23 Round to the nearest 10   (a) 36   (b) 62

24 Round to the nearest 100   (a) 455   (b) 719

25 Round 6548 to the nearest   (a) 10   (b) 100   (c) 1000

26 Write in Roman numbers: (a) 12   (b) 38   (c) 19

27 How much money?

28 (a) 27 + 19 + 8   (b) 34 + 29 + 16 + 17.

    Use a calculator to check your answers.

29 Draw a diagram to show how this moves
    FORWARD 20   RIGHT 90   FORWARD 30   LEFT 90   BACK 20

30 Draw a rectangle.   31 How many cubes?

32 Write down the next two

    (a) 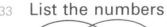   (b) 1 2 2 3 3 3 4 4 4

33 List the numbers   (a) in Set A   (b) in Set B

    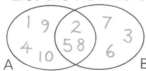   (c) in both Set A and Set B

                                     (d) in Set A but not in Set B.

34 The picture shows part of a thermometer.

What are the temperatures at

(a) **A,**   (b) **B,**   (c) **C?**

35 What time do these clocks show?

(a)   (b)

36 What will the time be

(a) 30 minutes after 4:48

(b) 20 minutes after 5:05?

37 A TV programme started at 6:50 and finished at 7:25.
How long was the programme?

38 Jill had . She bought some fruit for 27p.
How much money did she have left?

39 There are 10 biscuits in a packet.

(a) How many biscuits in 6 packets?

(b) How many biscuits will each child get when a packet
is shared equally by

(i) 2 children   (ii) 5 children?

40 Each stands for 5 apples.
Draw a picture to represent   (a) 20 apples   (b) 35 apples.

41 Write the fraction
that is coloured.

42 Write the fraction that is

(a) red   (b) not red.

43 A calculator is set to subtract 18 from any INPUT.

(a) What is the OUTPUT if 51 is entered?

(b) What was the INPUT if 46 is the OUTPUT?

44 Draw this shape

- - - - - - - - is the line of symmetry.
Draw the missing part of the shape.

45 Copy and complete

$$\begin{array}{r} R \\ 3\overline{)10} \\ \underline{} \\ \overline{} \end{array}$$

46 A box holds 10 chocolate eggs.

   (a) How many boxes will be filled if there are 48 eggs?

   (b) How many eggs will there be left?

47 What is the remainder, if any, when 35 is divided by

   (a) 2,   (b) 5,   (c) 10?

48 Write the odd numbers between 20 and 30.

49 Share 11 cakes equally between two people. How many each?

50 Write the answers: (a) $-5 +4 =$ (b) $-3 -2 =$

51 Measure this line to the nearest centimetre.

52 Copy and complete   53 What is the
                                     perimeter of
   (a) 4m = ____ cm   this shape?

   (b) 127cm = ____ m ____ cm.

54 How many millilitres equal one litre?

55 How many grams equal half a kilogram?

56 Ben drew ☐ to show 5 cars.
    How would he show 18 cars?

57 (a) What is the seventh month of the year?

   (b) What month is 5 months after June?

58 What day of the week is it

   (a) 4 days after Saturday

   (b) 5 days before Tuesday?

N
59 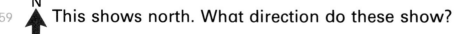 This shows north. What direction do these show?   (a)   (b)

60 What is the total cost of 4 books costing £8 each
    and 3 books costing £7 each?